CRIMCOMICS
LABELING THEORY

KRISTA S. GEHRING

WRITER

MICHAEL R. BATISTA

ARTIST

CHERYL L. WALLACE

LETTERER

OXFORD

UNIVERSITY PRESS

DEDICATION

To Cindy,

Thank you for all your love, support, and enthusiastic pride, especially when you say: "You did it all on your own!"

—KRISTA S. GEHRING

A special thanks to Ash, for being this issue's cover model.

—MICHAEL R. BATISTA

FOREWORD

CrimComics is a fresh take on the communication of criminology. Krista Gehring's script in this comic reflects a nuanced understanding of labeling theory. Michael Batista's artwork brings it to life with flair. Holistically that artistic grasp of the ideas is bound to help many students connect with the concepts. I learned from reading it and found it much more enjoyable to read than my own books on the subject!

This is true even though as a child I was not as enthusiastic about comics as most of my peers. That perhaps was because my parents managed a news agency in small-town Australia. We lived at the back of the shop. I frequently got the job of restoring order to the comics stand that had been disrupted by child comic enthusiasts. Stacking incoming comics was a form of child labor before I came to take an intellectual interest in comics.

We all learn in different ways. Which way works for us is a function of contingencies of our biographies as learners. I value Krista and Michael's work because it contributes a new path to learning. Shortcuts to learning are virtuous because they can whet young appetites to the high roads of learning. Just as a diagram in a textbook can be more educative than wads of text, so can pictures be worth a thousand words in a splendid publication like this one.

Labeling theory fell victim to premature positivism in criminology. Some influential literature reviews concluded that the evidence from quantitative studies infrequently detected statistically significant effects of labeling on lawbreaking. These measures of labeling did not show consistent consequences because they were measuring two different things that had opposite effects on crime.

What I defined more sharply as stigmatization makes crime worse. Stigmatization unfolds in the way the early labeling theorists suggested. Reintegrative shaming, on the other hand, reduced crime. In Cecilia Chouhy, Joshua C. Cochran, and Cheryl Lero Jonson's 2020 edited collection, *Criminal Justice Theory*, I updated the latest evidence from the discipline of psychology on why this is consistent with the labeling theory aspects of reintegrative shaming theory.

Even though reintegrative shaming was often measured as labeling in older studies, it did not label a person. It labeled criminality as bad, but criminals as good people who had done something bad. As the original labeling theorists taught us, a label must be prevented from becoming a master status trait. A master status trait defines the whole identity of a person as bad. Labels like junkie or criminal commonly did become a master status trait under the sentencing doctrine of stigmatization in western criminal law. This mistake of criminal law doctrine was reinforced by the way crime dramas on television stigmatized people with labels like junkie.

The hero cops who did that labeling were usually white, while those who were stigmatized were disproportionately black. Thankfully, that hidden curriculum of racism through the television script has improved somewhat in recent decades. Labeling theory has a message that emphasizes the importance of further movement away from that form of racism.

Premature rejection of labeling theory was a foolish mistake for criminology to make. It was based on quantitative criminological evidence that was myopic. This happened at a time when the qualitative research on delinquency and drift between different identities was so compelling. At that same point in the history of criminology when labeling theory was sidelined, the social identity tradition of research was becoming more central in the discipline of psychology. To put it crudely, this research showed that who we are is a set of identities we hold in our heads. So if our head tells us we are male, a farmer, an American, a Hillsong Christian, Trump supporter, and white, we are likely to think and behave differently than if our intelligence finds a contrary set of identities in our head.

In addition, when we do find First Nations people who commit a lot of crime, the evidence from many countries is that loss of identity is often a reason. Colonization and theft of their land, their language, and their buffalo stripped away identities. Rebuilding lost and healthy identities remains a future challenge for criminology. CHIME (connectedness, hope, identity, meaning, and empowerment) is imperative, as popularized in recent writing of British criminologist David Best. Best calls the journey toward retrieving CHIME as a search for recovery capital as a particular form of social capital. Restorative justice also aims at that recovery and CHIME. Krista Gehring and Michael Batista explain why.

Good restorative justice practice provides for a celebration circle of reintegration and love once an effort has been made to heal the harm. The celebration circle celebrates the CHIME a victim, an offender, and a community have found through their own agency, through active responsibility for righting the wrong. That also connects the restorative justice tradition of thinking about social capital with the collective efficacy tradition that comes from the Chicago School of sociology, as exemplified by Robert Sampson's work, and as discussed in another *CrimComics* (Issue 4).

Restorative justice seeks to avert labeling and stigma by putting the problem, not the person, in the center of the circle of citizen deliberation over a crime. Children are not born democratic. First Nations' children are not born with a healthy tribal identity, group identity, or intersectoral gender identity. They can nevertheless learn to be democratic in a restorative circle through the practical work of CHIME that heals harms.

Enjoy work you value through your comics. Have fun with serious matters and then you will make better contributions to resolving them. There lies the value in the uplifting work of Krista Gehring and Michael Batista.

JOHN BRAITHWAITE
Australian National University

PREFACE

We live in a world dominated by labels. We categorize ourselves and each other using terms that indicate our group affiliations, political ideologies, occupations, social roles, religion, economic status, struggles, triumphs, and much more. While many of these labels may allow us to make sense of the world, labels can also lead to harmful unintended consequences. Labels reflect and affect how we and others think about our identities as well as how we think about ourselves, and if these labels are negative, this can lead to damaging self-fulfilling prophecies.

When I talk to students about the theories presented in this issue, I ask them if they had "that classmate" or "that person in the neighborhood" who was labeled a "bad kid." Did your parents warn you not to play with that child? Did the teachers react to that child differently than they did to the "good students"? Was the child immediately blamed when something bad happened? Did that child end up acting out and doing more "bad things" as time went on? Inevitably, my students will nod and smile, as I think we all have known "that kid" at some point in our lives. But what if the response to the child's bad behavior had been one of labeling the behavior as bad, not the child? Imagine how different the interactions that child would have had with others, and how he/she/they would have been viewed by family, friends, teachers, and other individuals. Words matter, and what we say about others and ourselves makes a lasting impact.

This is true of individuals who are in the criminal justice system. We label them as "criminals," "offenders," "felons," "inmates," "convicts," and many other terms that make their experience their identity. Labeling theory focuses on society's reaction to deviance. Indeed, these labels impact how others see these individuals and often impede their access to resources (i.e., employment, housing, loans) well after their sentence has been served. Labeling theory acknowledges this phenomenon and proposes that the very thing that is supposed to prevent criminal behavior (i.e., state intervention) actually creates it.

In the United States, once one acquires a label of "criminal" or "offender," there is also a degree of shame that comes with that identity. Here, the criminal justice system engages in stigmatic or disintegrative shaming, and this can destroy the bond between the individual and the community. Shame can be a powerful force that impacts many aspects of a person's identity and how he/she/they are perceived by and relate to others. Conversely, reintegrative shaming, a practice that acknowledges that the *behavior* was wrong (not the individual), tries to reintegrate the individual back into the community. One wonders if there could ever be a shift to this practice in American society, as we seem to be stuck in our ways of shaming and labeling others. There has been some movement toward reintegration by using restorative justice conferences, but it will likely be a long time before there is a notable shift in the system from one of shame to one of support.

As with any book project, *CrimComics* consumed much time and effort, perhaps more so than a traditional textbook. Thinking about theory—and, in particular, trying to design a work that best conveys the theories in a visual medium—is fun. Still, with busy lives, finding the space in one's day to carefully research, write, illustrate, ink, and letter the pages of this work is a source of some stress. We were fortunate, however, to have had an amazing amount of support during these times from family, friends, and Oxford University Press. We also want to acknowledge the talents of Cheryl Wallace. Cheryl's flair for lettering allowed us to get our ideas across to the readers.

The support of these and so many other individuals has made creating *CrimComics* possible and a rewarding experience for us. We would like to thank the following reviewers: Daniel Reinhard, Texas State University; Elizabeth B Perkins, Morehead State University; Joshua Long, University of MA-Lowell; Michaela Soyer, Hunter College; Michelle D. Miranda, Farmingdale State College; Molly McDowell, Texas State University; Timbre Wulf, University of Nebraska at Kearney; Wade Jacobsen, University of Maryland. We hope that this and other issues of *CrimComics* will inspire in your students a passion to learn criminological theory.

Labeling Theory

MOST THEORIES THAT DISCUSS WHY CRIME HAPPENS TEND TO FOCUS EITHER ON EXPLAINING WHY AN INDIVIDUAL ENGAGES IN CRIMINAL BEHAVIOR OR HOW A SOCIAL ENVIRONMENT OR CIRCUMSTANCE CONTRIBUTES TO CRIME RATES.

LABELING THEORY TAKES A DIFFERENT APPROACH: IT PROPOSES THAT THE VERY THING THAT IS USED TO PREVENT AND REDUCE CRIME-- STATE INTERVENTION-- ACTUALLY CAUSES IT.

THIS THEORY QUESTIONS WHY SOME ACTS ARE LABELED "CRIMINAL" AND OTHERS ARE NOT...

...AND WHY SOME PEOPLE LABELED ARE "CRIMINAL" AND OTHERS ARE NOT.

WHILE CRIME IS DEFINED AS "BEHAVIOR THAT VIOLATES CRIMINAL LAW," LABELING THEORISTS ARGUE THAT CRIME IS A SOCIALLY CONSTRUCTED PHENOMENON.

WHAT IS OR IS NOT VIEWED AS "CRIMINAL" CHANGES OVER TIME, DEPENDS ON PLACE, AND OFTEN VARIES BY SOCIETY OR CULTURE.

THEY EVEN SUGGEST THAT THE IDEA THAT SOME BEHAVIORS ARE FUNDAMENTALLY CRIMINAL IS NOT NECESSARILY TRUE.

FOR EXAMPLE, HOMICIDE IS THE KILLING OF ONE HUMAN BEING BY ANOTHER. SOME ACTS ARE CONSIDERED CRIMES...

...WHILE OTHERS ARE PERMITTED, RARELY PROSECUTED AS CRIMES, OR ARE EVEN DIRECTED BY THE LEGAL SYSTEM.

WHAT DIFFERS FOR THESE ACTS IS THE
SOCIETAL REACTIONS TO THE KILLING.

LABELING THEORISTS CLAIM THAT STATE
INTERVENTION IS "DANGEROUSLY
CRIMINOGENIC" IN THAT THE LABELS
WE PLACE ON INDIVIDUALS WHO COMMIT
CRIMES CAN LEAD THEM TO CONTINUE
TO ENGAGE IN CRIMINAL BEHAVIOR.

EX-CON CONVICT

FELON

MURDERER

CRIMINAL

THUG

OUTLAW

HOODLUM

LIFER

INMATE

PRISONER

GANGSTER

CROOK!

jailbird HOOLIGAN

LOSER

EVIL

IN THE LATE 1930S, LABELING THEORY EMERGED AS AN EXPLANATION FOR CRIME AND CRIMINAL BEHAVIOR IN THE FIELD OF CRIMINOLOGY.

AT THAT TIME, PRESIDENT ROOSEVELT HAD IMPLEMENTED VARIOUS PROGRAMS DURING HIS "NEW DEAL" TO PULL THE UNITED STATES OUT OF THE GREAT DEPRESSION.

I PLEDGE YOU, I PLEDGE MYSELF, TO A NEW DEAL FOR THE AMERICAN PEOPLE.

HE TOOK RESPONSIBILITY FOR THE OUTSTANDING PERFORMANCE OF THE ECONOMY THAT WAS SLOWLY RECOVERING FROM THE GREAT DEPRESSION.

YOU CANT GET FAT on a FIRESIDE CHAT!

HOWEVER, THE AMERICAN ECONOMY TOOK A SHARP DOWNTURN IN 1937 THAT MADE MANY BELIEVE ROOSEVELT'S NEW DEAL POLICIES WERE TO BLAME. FOR EXAMPLE, THOUSANDS OF PEOPLE LOST THEIR JOBS WHEN GOVERNMENT PROGRAMS LIKE THE WORKS PROGRESS ADMINISTRATION LAID THEM OFF. THEREFORE, IF THE GOVERNMENT WAS RESPONSIBLE FOR THE PROSPERITY, IT MUST ALSO BE RESPONSIBLE FOR THIS HARDSHIP. THE PUBLIC HAD GROWN DISILLUSIONED WITH THE GOVERNMENT AND DID NOT TRUST THAT IT WAS ACTING ON THE BEST INTEREST OF THE PEOPLE.

THIS SOCIAL CONTEXT PROVIDED AN IDEAL ENVIRONMENT TO PROPOSE THAT STATE INTERVENTION WITH LAWBREAKERS WAS DOING MORE HARM THAN GOOD. IN 1938, **FRANK TANNENBAUM** PUT FORTH IDEAS THAT SHAPED THE FOUNDATION OF LABELING THEORY IN CRIMINOLOGY. THE THEORY EMERGED OUT OF TANNENBAUM'S STUDIES OF THE CRIMINOLOGICAL RESEARCH AT THAT TIME...

...AND HIS OWN PERSONAL EXPERIENCE WITH STATE INTERVENTION.*

*TANNENBAUM WAS ARRESTED AND INCARCERATED ON SEVERAL OCCASIONS DUE TO HIS INVOLVEMENT WITH THE INDUSTRIAL WORKERS OF THE WORLD, AN INTERNATIONAL LABOR UNION.

IN HIS WORK CRIME AND THE COMMUNITY (1938), TANNENBAUM PROPOSED HIS THEORY OF **"THE DRAMA-TIZATION OF EVIL."**

TANNENBAUM PROPOSED THAT ONLY SOME INDIVIDUALS WHO BREAK THE LAW ARE CAUGHT.

GOTCHA! YA THINK YOU'RE GOING TO JUST TAKE THAT WITHOUT PAYING, HUH?

AN ARREST SINGLES THE PERSON OUT FOR DIFFERENTIAL TREATMENT AND EXPOSES HIM TO VARIOUS SYSTEMS AND CIRCUMSTANCES THAT OTHERS DO NOT EXPERIENCE.

K 38 937

THE PERSON'S WORLD IS ALTERED...

...PEOPLE REACT DIFFERENTLY TO HIM OR HER...

BILLY, I DON'T WANT YOU PLAYING WITH HIM--HE'S A THIEF!

...AND THE PERSON STARTS TO RECONSIDER HIS OR HER IDENTITY.

EVERYONE THINKS I'M A THIEF, A CROOK...

MAYBE I REALLY AM?

MAYBE THAT'S MY DESTINY?

TANNENBAUM INTRODUCED THE IDEA OF *TAGGING*.

DURING HIS RESEARCH, HE FOUND THAT WHEN A JUVENILE WAS GIVEN A NEGATIVE TAG OR LABEL, THIS OFTEN CONTRIBUTED TO FUTURE PARTICIPATION IN DELINQUENT BEHAVIORS.

THE YOUNGSTER MAY GET INVOLVED WITH A JUVENILE GANG TO MEET VARIOUS PSYCHOLOGICAL NEEDS FOR PLAY, ADVENTURE, AND FUN.

OFFICER, YOU REALLY NEED TO DO SOMETHING ABOUT THOSE BOYS. THEY ARE GAMBLING AND CAUSING TROUBLE--THEY ARE NOTHING BUT RIFFRAFF.

THE COMMUNITY'S DISAPPROVAL OF THEIR ACTIVITIES ULTIMATELY LEADS THE JUVENILES TO RESENT THE SOCIAL REJECTION.

THE JUVENILES OFTEN BECOME AWARE OF THIS REJECTION DUE TO GAINING A BAD REPUTATION, A CRIMINAL LABEL, OR A COMBINATION OF BOTH.

GET BACK HERE, YOU CROOKS!

TANNENBAUM PROPOSED THAT THE FIRST ENCOUNTER WITH THE CRIMINAL JUSTICE SYSTEM, THAT IS, THE VERY FIRST "DRAMATIZATION OF 'EVIL,'" PLAYED A TREMENDOUS ROLE IN MAKING THE PERSON A "CRIMINAL", PERHAPS MORE THAN ANY OTHER EXPERIENCE. THAT IS, THE DELINQUENT BECAME BAD BECAUSE HE WAS LABELED AS "BAD."

IN *COMMUNITY AND CRIME* (1938), HE PROPOSED THAT THE DRAMATIZATION OF EVIL INVOLVED "A PROCESS OF TAGGING, DEFINING, IDENTIFYING, SEGREGATING, DESCRIBING, EMPHASIZING, MAKING CONSCIOUS AND SELF-CONSCIOUS; IT BECOMES A WAY OF STIMULATING, SUGGESTING, EMPHASIZING, AND EVOKING THE VERY TRAITS THAT ARE COMPLAINED OF" (P. 19).

AS THE SOCIAL CONTEXT CONTINUED TO CHANGE, SOCIETY'S VIEWS ABOUT CRIME AND CRIMINALS CHANGED AS WELL.

THE SECOND WORLD WAR (WWII) BEGAN IN 1939 WHEN NAZI GERMANY, UNDER ADOLF HITLER, INVADED POLAND.

WWII BROUGHT ABOUT AN INDUSTRIAL MOBILIZATION IN WHICH FACTORIES BEGAN PRODUCING PRODUCTS FOR THE WAR. THIS AND THE RESULTING INCREASES IN EMPLOYMENT LED TO THE END OF THE GREAT DEPRESSION.

THE UNITED STATES BECAME INVOLVED IN WWII SHORTLY AFTER THE ATTACK ON PEARL HARBOR ON DECEMBER 7, 1941.

IN GENERAL, CRIME RATES IN THE UNITED STATES DROPPED DURING WWII.

THIS WAS LIKELY DUE TO THE REMOVAL OF A LARGE PROPORTION OF YOUNG MEN INTO THE ARMED SERVICES AND TO THE GROWING ECONOMIC PROSPERITY BROUGHT ABOUT BY WARTIME ECONOMY.

WHEN THE WAR ENDED IN 1945, AMERICANS BELIEVED IN THE SUPERIORITY OF THE UNITED STATES BECAUSE IT HAD EMERGED AS ONE OF THE TWO DOMINANT SUPERPOWERS (ALONG WITH THE SOVIET UNION).

THE ECONOMY WAS BOOMING, AND THE NEWLY EMERGING MIDDLE CLASS BECAME OBSESSED WITH BUYING CONSUMER GOODS.

THE MIAMI HERALD

WAR ENDS

FAMILIES WERE MOVING TO THE NEWLY FORMED SUBURBS, AND TRADITIONAL GENDER ROLES WERE REAFFIRMED ONCE AGAIN.

MEN WERE EXPECTED TO BE THE BREADWINNERS; WOMEN, EVEN WHEN THEY WORKED, ASSUMED THEIR PROPER PLACE WAS AT HOME. CONFORMITY AND UNIFORMITY WERE ENCOURAGED AND ENFORCED.

ANYONE WHO DID NOT FIT THAT MOLD WAS VIEWED WITH SUSPICION.

IN 1951, *EDWIN LEMERT* WROTE *SOCIAL PATHOLOGY.* HE BUILT UPON TANNENBAUM'S IDEAS AND DESIGNATED TWO TYPES OF DEVIANCE. HE PROVIDED A MORE COMPLETE DISCUSSION OF THE PROCESS BY WHICH A PERSON'S BEHAVIORS LED TO HIS OR HER LABELING AND POSSIBLE EXCLUSION FROM LARGER SOCIETY.

PRIMARY DEVIANCE OCCURS WHEN A PERSON ENGAGES IN THE INITIAL ACT OF DEVIANCE.

STEVEN? WERE YOU OUT DRINKING AGAIN?

AH, IT'S NO BIG DEAL, MOM. WE WERE JUST HAVING FUN.

WHILE THIS PRIMARY DEVIANCE IS RECOGNIZED AS UNDESIRABLE, IT DOES NOT HAVE AN IMPACT ON THE STATUS OR SELF-IMAGE OF THE DEVIANT.

NOW, YOU KIDS KNOW YOU SHOULDN'T BE DOING THIS.

I WANT YOU TO POUR OUT YOUR BEERS AND GET ON HOME.

AW, OKAY, OFFICER ARBOGAST.

THE PERSON OFTEN RATIONALIZES HIS DEVIANT BEHAVIOR AS A TEMPORARY BAD ACT OR SEES IT AS PART OF A SOCIALLY ACCEPTABLE ROLE.

WE WERE LUCKY THIS WEEKEND THAT WE DIDN'T GET BUSTED BY THE COPS!

I KNOW! IT'S NOT LIKE WE WERE DOING ANYTHING *REALLY* BAD. EVERYONE DRINKS--AND WE DON'T DO IT ALL THE TIME.

THE PERSON DOESN'T SEE HIMSELF AS DEVIANT OR CRIMINAL, AND HE DOESN'T ORGANIZE HIS LIFE AROUND THIS IDENTITY.

SECONDARY DEVIANCE OCCURS WHEN OTHERS RESPOND TO THE INITIAL DEVIANT ACT (PRIMARY DEVIANCE).

I'M TIRED OF TELLING YOU KIDS TO STOP DRINKING--YOU'RE ALL UNDER ARREST!

I CAN'T BELIEVE THIS, STEVEN. ARRESTED? I TOLD YOU TO STOP DRINKING WITH YOUR FRIENDS!

YOU ARE GOING TO TURN OUT TO BE A DRUNK, JUST LIKE YOUR FATHER!

AS SOCIETAL REACTION INTENSIFIES WITH EACH ACT OF PRIMARY DEVIANCE, THE PERSON BECOMES STIGMATIZED THROUGH "NAME CALLING, LABELING, OR STEREOTYPING."

I DON'T KNOW WHAT IT'S GOING TO TAKE TO GET THESE KIDS TO STOP.

I'VE ARRESTED THIS KID LIKE TEN TIMES IN THE PAST TWO MONTHS.

THE PERSON REACTS TO THE STIGMATIZING LABELS AND HARSHER PENALTIES BY INCREASING AND REINFORCING HIS DEVIANT CONDUCT.

SECONDARY DEVIANCE CAN BE SO STRONG THAT THE PERSON ADOPTS A *MASTER STATUS*. A MASTER STATUS DESCRIBES THE CHIEF CHARAC-TERISTIC OF AN INDIVIDUAL, AND THE PERSON ORGANIZES HIS LIFE AROUND THIS IDENTITY.

NOW THAT HE HAS BEEN LABELED, HE BEGINS TO DEVELOP A REPUTATION THAT FITS THAT LABEL. HE EMBRACES HIS DEVIANT IDENTITY AND STARTS ACTING OUT EVEN MORE, BREAKING MORE AND MORE RULES.

AS THE '50S DECADE PROGRESSED, THE CHILDREN BORN DURING THE EARLY YEARS OF THE POSTWAR "BABY BOOM" WERE BECOMING TEENAGERS.

THE RAPID RISE OF THIS NEW DEMOGRAPHIC AND THE BOOMING ECONOMY LED TO TEENAGERS HAVING MORE LEISURE TIME AND SIGNIFICANT SPENDING POWER.

THIS POWER OF THE EMERGING TEEN DEMOGRAPHIC CAUSED MORE ANXIETY FOR THE OLDER GENERATIONS AS TEENAGERS APPEARED TO BE CHALLENGING THE STATUS QUO.

THERE WAS A BELIEF THAT ROCK AND ROLL, COMICS, MOVIES, AND OTHER THINGS TEENS WERE BUYING AND ENJOYING WERE TO BLAME FOR MISBEHAVIOR OF THIS GROUP.

THE COMIC BOOKS, INTENT AND EFFECT, ARE DE-MORALIZING THE MORALS OF THE YOUTH. THEY ARE SEXUALLY AGGRESSIVE IN AN ABNORMAL WAY. THEY MAKE VIOLENCE ALLURING AND CRUELTY HEROIC.

THE NUMBER OF CRIMES COMMITTED BY TEENAGERS WAS, IN FACT, RISING THROUGHOUT THE NATION.

IT WAS SUCH A CONCERN THAT THE UNITED STATES SENATE HAD SUBCOMMITTEE HEARINGS REGARDING THE CAUSES OF JUVENILE DELINQUENCY.

THE MOST WELL KNOWN WAS THE 1954 COMIC BOOK HEARINGS.

THERE WERE MORE EXTREME CASES
OF TEENAGE VIOLENCE HAPPENING
AS THE DECADE CAME TO A CLOSE.

IN 1958, 19-YEAR-OLD CHARLES
STARKWEATHER WENT ON A TWO-MONTH
MURDER SPREE, KILLING 11 PEOPLE IN
THE MIDWEST. HE WAS ACCOMPANIED BY HIS
14-YEAR-OLD GIRLFRIEND, CARIL ANN FUGATE.

IN 1960, A PUBLIC OPINION POLL FOUND THAT
JUVENILE DELINQUENCY WAS RANKED THIRD
AMONG AMERICAN'S GREATEST CONCERNS,
AFTER NATIONAL DEFENSE AND WORLD PEACE.

BUT THE EARLY 1960S WAS ALSO
A TIME OF GREAT OPTIMISM.

JOHN F. KENNEDY WAS SWORN
IN AS THE 35TH PRESIDENT
OF THE UNITED STATES IN 1961.

HE PROPOSED THAT AMERICANS SHOULD BE A
UNITED PEOPLE, ACTIVE CITIZENS FIGHTING
AGAINST SOCIAL ILLS LIKE POVERTY AND TYRANNY.

ASK NOT
WHAT YOUR
COUNTRY
CAN DO FOR YOU.
ASK WHAT YOU CAN
DO FOR YOUR
COUNTRY.

ON NOVEMBER 22, 1963, WHEN KENNEDY WAS ASSASSINATED, LYNDON B. JOHNSON WAS SWORN IN AS THE PRESIDENT OF THE UNITED STATES. HE WON THE PRESIDENTIAL ELECTION A YEAR LATER.

HE HAD A VISION TO BUILD "A GREAT SOCIETY" FOR THE AMERICAN PEOPLE.

FINAL

DAILY NEWS
NEW YORK'S PICTURE NEWSPAPER

7¢

Vol. 46. No. 166

New York, N.Y.

LBJ'S BLUEPRINT
Billions for Schools, Aged; Medicare & War on Poverty

The State of the

president pro tem of the Senate. T

THE "GREAT SOCIETY" WAS A SET OF DOMESTIC PROGRAMS THAT WERE AIMED AT WIPING OUT POVERTY, CRIME, AND RACIAL INJUSTICE.

JOHNSON SIGNED SEVERAL IMPORTANT ACTS DURING THE FIRST YEAR OF HIS PRESIDENCY THAT HAD A MAJOR IMPACT ON EDUCATION, HEALTH, AND POVERTY WITH THE HOPES OF WAGING WHAT HE CALLED A "*WAR ON POVERTY*."

THIS POLITICAL AGENDA REAFFIRMED THAT THE GOVERNMENT SHOULD STEP IN AND TAKE CARE OF SOCIAL ILLS BY IMPLEMENTING PROGRAMS TO EFFECT CHANGE.

THE GOVERNMENT COULD BE TRUSTED TO DO WHAT'S BEST FOR ITS CITIZENS.

BUT SEVERAL CRISES WERE BREWING THAT MADE CITIZENS BEGIN TO MIS-TRUST THE GOVERNMENT'S INTENTIONS AND BELIEVE THERE WAS ABUSE OF POWER.

BEGINNING IN 1964, THERE WERE MULTIPLE RACE RIOTS THAT OCCURRED IN CITIES LIKE HARLEM, WATTS, AND NEWARK THAT INVOLVED AFRICAN-AMERICANS ACTING AGAINST SYMBOLS OF WHITE SOCIETY, AUTHORITY, AND PROPERTY IN THEIR NEIGHBORHOODS.

THIS RAGE WAS FUELED BY POLICE PRACTICES, UNEMPLOYMENT AND UNDEREMPLOYMENT, AND INADEQUATE HOUSING.

WHETHER IT WAS A VIOLENT RIOT OR A PEACEFUL PROTEST, WHEN GOVERNMENT OFFICIALS ARRIVED, CITIZENS WERE OFTEN BEATEN AND BRUTALIZED BY THEM.

IN ADDITION TO TURMOIL AT HOME, THE UNITED STATES INCREASED MILITARY INVOLVEMENT IN THE VIETNAM WAR IN 1964.

SOON, THE UNITED STATES LAUNCHED A LARGE-SCALE BOMBING CAMPAIGN AGAINST NORTH VIETNAMESE TARGETS THAT LASTED FOR MORE THAN TWO YEARS.

PRESIDENT JOHNSON ALSO AUTHORIZED THE DEPLOYMENT OF GROUND TROOPS TO FIGHT THE VIET CONG IN THE VIETNAMESE COUNTRYSIDE.

THE WAR ON POVERTY WAS ULTIMATELY LIMITED IN ITS EFFECTIVENESS AS MORE RESOURCES WERE DIVERTED TO THE INVOLVEMENT IN THE VIETNAM WAR.

CHICAGO, 1968. DEMOCRATIC NATIONAL CONVENTION.

MANY CITIZENS OPPOSED THE UNITED STATES' INVOLVEMENT IN THE VIETNAM WAR, AND SEVERAL ANTIWAR PROTESTS RESULTED IN LOCAL LAW ENFORCEMENT AND THE NATIONAL GUARD ENGAGING IN VIOLENT CONFRONTATIONS WITH PROTESTORS.

IN 1970, THE NATIONAL GUARD OPENED FIRE ON ANTIWAR PROTESTORS AT KENT STATE UNIVERSITY, KILLING FOUR COLLEGE STUDENTS AND INJURING NINE OTHERS.

IN 1971, INMATES IN NEW YORK'S MAXIMUM SECURITY ATTICA CORRECTIONAL FACILITY TOOK CONTROL OF THE INSTITUTION AND TOOK MEMBERS OF THE PRISON STAFF HOSTAGE TO DEMAND IMPROVED LIVING CONDITIONS.

AFTER FOUR DAYS OF NEGOTIATIONS WITH THE INMATES, STATE POLICE OFFICERS STORMED THE PRISON, KILLING 29 INMATES AND 10 HOSTAGES.

FROM 1972 TO 1974, THE WATERGATE SCANDAL ENGULFED THE NIXON ADMINISTRATION, ULTIMATELY LEADING TO RICHARD NIXON'S RESIGNATION.

...BECAUSE PEOPLE HAVE GOT TO KNOW WHETHER OR NOT THEIR PRESIDENT IS A CROOK. WELL, I AM NOT A CROOK.

THESE AND OTHER EVENTS LED MANY TO LOSE THEIR CONFIDENCE IN THE INTENTIONS OR COMPETENCE OF GOVERNMENT OFFICIALS.

THE 1960S PROVIDED A SOCIAL CONTEXT FOR CRIMINOLOGISTS TO EMBRACE IDEAS FROM LABELING THEORIES THAT BLAMED THE STATE FOR THE CRIME PROBLEM.

HUGE C.I.A. OPERATION REPORTED IN U.S. AGAINST ANTIWAR FORCES, OTHER DISSIDENTS IN NIXON YEARS

FILES ON CITIZE

IDEAS CAUSE REACTIONS.

Helms Reportedly Got Surveillance Data in

IF, ACCORDING TO LABELING THEORIES, STATE INTERVENTION CAUSES CRIME, POLICIES SHOULD BE IMPLEMENTED THAT DECREASE OR ELIMINATE STATE INTERVENTION.

DECRIMINALIZATION CAN DECREASE STATE INTERVENTION BY REMOVING MANY FORMS OF CONDUCT FROM CRIMINAL LAW.

FOR EXAMPLE, INSTEAD OF TREATING THE ACTS AS CRIMINAL WITH HEFTY SANCTIONS AND/OR EXTENSIVE INVOLVEMENT WITH THE CRIMINAL JUSTICE SYSTEM, THE ACTS MAY BE TREATED SIMILARLY TO TRAFFIC VIOLATIONS WITH PENALTIES LIKE MINOR FINES.

IT COULD ALSO INVOLVE COMPLETE *LEGALIZATION* OF THE ACT. DECRIMINAL-IZATION IS OFTEN DISCUSSED REGARDING ACTS LIKE DRUG USE, GAMBLING, AND SEX WORK.

MANY *DIVERSION* PROGRAMS HAVE BEEN CREATED TO DIVERT INDIVIDUALS FROM THE CRIMINAL JUSTICE SYSTEM IN ORDER TO AVOID NEGATIVE CONSEQUENCES OF A CRIMINAL CONVICTION.

ONE TYPE OF DIVERSION PROGRAM--*SPECIALTY COURTS, TREATMENT COURTS*, OR *PROBLEM-SOLVING COURTS*--HAS BECOME COMMONPLACE IN THE CRIMINAL JUSTICE SYSTEM.

THESE COURTS HAVE SPECIALIZED DOCKETS THAT SEEK TO ADDRESS THE UNDERLYING PROBLEM(S) CONTRIBUTING TO CERTAIN CRIMINAL OFFENSES. THE PROGRAM GENERALLY INVOLVES COORDINATING THE EFFORTS OF THE JUDGE, PROSECUTOR, DEFENSE ATTORNEY, PROBATION, LAW ENFORCEMENT, MENTAL HEALTH SERVICES, AND SOCIAL SERVICE AGENCIES TO HELP THE DEFENDANT.

EXAMPLES INCLUDE DRUG COURTS, MENTAL HEALTH COURTS, VETERANS COURTS, DUI COURTS, HOMELESS COURTS, AND PROSTITUTION COURTS.

LABELING THEORISTS HAVE ALSO CALLED FOR EXPANDING *DUE PROCESS*, WHICH SEEKS TO PROVIDE LEGAL PROTECTIONS TO INDIVIDUALS WHO ARE ACCUSED OF CRIMES.

THIS IS BASED ON A GROWING DISTRUST OF OFFICIALS LIKE THE POLICE, JUDGES, AND PAROLE BOARDS, WHO HAVE WIDE DISCRETION REGARDING JUSTICE-INVOLVED INDIVIDUALS.

LABELING THEORISTS ALSO BELIEVED THAT INCARCERATION CONTRIBUTED TO CRIMINAL BEHAVIOR, AS PEOPLE WHO WENT TO PRISON OFTEN BECAME WORSE WHILE THEY WERE THERE.

THIS LED THEM TO ADVOCATE FOR REDUCING PRISON POPULATIONS THROUGH *DEINSTITUTIONALIZATION*.

THEY CALLED FOR AN END TO NEW PRISON CONSTRUCTION AND MORE WAYS FOR INDIVIDUALS TO SERVE THEIR SENTENCES IN THE COMMUNITY.

DUE TO REDUCED STATE BUDGETS AND FEWER AND FEWER CALLS TO GET "TOUGH ON CRIME," MANY STATES HAVE IMPLEMENTED POLICIES TO REDUCE THEIR PRISON POPULATION.

LAWSUITS HAVE ALSO BEEN FILED TO COMBAT PRISON OVERCROWDING. FOR EXAMPLE, *BROWN V. PLATA (2011)* FOUND THAT CROWDING IN CALIFORNIA'S PRISONS VIOLATED THE EIGHTH AMENDMENT AND MANDATED THE RELEASE OF TENS OF THOUSANDS OF INMATES.

RESEARCH FOUND THAT IN GENERAL, THIS AND OTHER DEINSTITUTIONALIZATION POLICIES DID NOT ENDANGER PUBLIC SAFETY OR LEAD TO INCREASED CRIME RATES.

THERE HAVE BEEN EXTENSIONS OF LABELING THEORY THAT DELVE INTO HOW SANCTIONS MAY IMPACT CRIMINAL BEHAVIOR.

SOME THEORISTS BEGAN TO PROPOSE THAT THE ISSUE WAS NOT JUST WHETHER A SANCTION WAS APPLIED, BUT THE QUALITY OF THE SANCTION WAS IMPORTANT TOO.

ONE THEORIST, **JOHN BRAITHWAITE**, FOCUSED ON THE CONCEPT OF **SHAME** AND HOW THIS IMPACTED CONTINUED CRIMINAL INVOLVEMENT.

SHAMING HAS BEEN USED AS A FORM OF SOCIAL CONTROL; IT OCCURS WHEN A PERSON VIOLATES THE NORMS OF THE COMMUNITY, AND OTHER PEOPLE RESPOND BY PUBLICLY CRITICIZING, AVOIDING, OR OSTRACIZING HIM.

WHEN THE JURY SEES THE PERP LAUGHING AND JOKING--THAT PUTS A BAD TASTE IN THEIR MOUTH...

SHAME LEADS US TO LABEL THE PERSON AS BAD, NOT JUST THE BEHAVIOR.

...OH, GOTTA LOOK GOOD FOR THE CAMERA, I GUESS! I THINK HE IS TAKING THIS VERY LIGHTLY. I DON'T THINK HE BELIEVES HE IS GOING TO BE CONVICTED.

FIFTEEN YEARS LATER.

IN HIS BOOK *CRIME, SHAME, AND REINTEGRATION* (1989), BRAITHWAITE DISCUSSED WHICH SOCIAL REACTION (I.E., TYPE OF SHAMING) RESULTS IN MORE OR LESS CRIMINAL BEHAVIOR.

HI, RICKY! HOW WAS THE JOB SEARCH TODAY?

NOT SO GOOD, ANGELA. ALL THE JOB APPLICATIONS WANTED TO KNOW IF I HAD BEEN CONVICTED OF A FELONY.

STIGMATIZATION OR ***DISINTEGRATIVE SHAMING*** IS CONSISTENT WITH LABELING THEORY, AS THE SHAMING STIGMATIZES AND EXCLUDES THE PERSON FROM THE COMMUNITY.

I DON'T KNOW WHAT I'M GOING TO DO, ANGELA. THIS CONVICTION HAS MADE ME LOSE SO MUCH--WHEN I WAS IN PRISON, I LOST MY FREEDOM.

I LOST FIFTEEN YEARS OF MY LIFE!

NOW THAT I'M OUT, I'M LOSING OPPORTUNITIES. IT'S LIKE MY SENTENCE WILL NEVER END.

STIGMATIZATION IS DISRESPECTFUL SHAMING AND TREATS THE INDIVIDUAL AS THOUGH HE OR SHE IS A BAD PERSON. IT IS UNFORGIVING AND PERMANENTLY LABELS HIM OR HER.

PEOPLE WON'T HIRE ME. I CAN'T APPLY FOR FEDERAL OR STATE GRANTS TO GO TO SCHOOL. I CAN'T LIVE IN PUBLIC HOUSING, OR RECEIVE FEDERAL CASH ASSISTANCE, SSI, OR FOOD STAMPS...

THESE COLLATERAL CONSEQUENCES OF IMPRISONMENT OFTEN CAUSE FORMERLY INCARCERATED INDIVIDUALS TO RETURN TO THEIR PREVIOUS BEHAVIORS.

YO, RICKY! I HEARD YOU WERE OUT! WANNA GO FOR A RIDE?

THE PERSON IS BRANDED AN OUTCAST BECAUSE HE CANNOT BOND WITH CONVENTIONAL SOCIETY, SO HE JOINS A CRIMINAL SUBCULTURE.

IN THE CRIMINAL SUBCULTURE, THERE ARE MANY OPPORTUNITIES TO BREAK THE LAW AND CRIMINALITY IS REINFORCED. THE OPPORTUNITIES TO "SUCCEED" ARE PLENTIFUL, AND CRIMINAL BEHAVIOR IS APPEALING AS IT PROVIDES A MEANS TO SURVIVE AND EXCEL IN WAYS CONVENTIONAL SOCIETY DID NOT PROVIDE.

WE'RE GOING TO VISIT A GUY WHO OWES ME SOME MONEY. YOU READY?

THUS, STIGMATIZATION INCREASES CRIME.

BRAITHWAITE ALSO DISCUSSES ANOTHER TYPE OF SHAMING IN HIS WORK: *REINTEGRATIVE SHAMING*.

ASH! ASH! PLAY THE "GOOSE GAME" WITH ME.

NO, OLLY, I'M PLAYING FORTNITE. I DON'T WANT TO PLAY THE "GOOSE GAME".

THE BEST PLACE TO OBSERVE THIS TYPE OF SHAMING IS IN LOVING FAMILIES.

ASH, YOU ALWAYS PLAY THAT GAME! I WANT TO PLAY!

I SAID *NO!*

ASHTON! DID YOU HURT YOUR BROTHER?

IT IS EXPECTED THAT OFFENSES WILL OCCUR IN A FAMILY.

THAT'S IT-- NO MORE VIDEO GAMES. GO TO YOUR ROOM, YOUNG MAN.

WHEN A CHILD IS PUNISHED, HE OR SHE IS NOT LABELED A "CRIMINAL CHILD" OR REMOVED FROM THE FAMILY TO LIVE IN ISOLATION.

THE CHILD GETS HIS PUNISHMENT WITHIN A CONTINUUM OF LOVE AND IS TREATED AS AN INDIVIDUAL WHO MADE A MISTAKE.

WHEN THE CHILD IS PUNISHED, BOTH PARENT AND CHILD KNOW THAT AFTERWARD THEY WILL GO ON LIVING TOGETHER AS THEY DID BEFORE.

USING THIS "FAMILY MODEL" TO DEAL WITH JUSTICE-INVOLVED INDIVIDUALS INVOLVES EXPRESSING DIS-APPROVAL WHILE SUSTAINING A RELATIONSHIP OF RESPECT AND LABELING THE BEHAVIOR AS DEVIANT, NOT THE INDIVIDUAL.

WHILE THE PERSON MAY HAVE BEHAVED IN A WAY THAT OFFENDED THE COMMUNITY, THE BEHAVIOR IS ADDRESSED AND THEN THE PERSON IS REINTEGRATED BACK INTO THE COMMUNITY THROUGH WORDS OR GESTURES OF FORGIVENESS.

TYPICALLY, SANCTIONS EXACT RETRIBUTION FOR THE VICTIM AND THE LARGER COMMUNITY BY INFLICTING SOME SORT OF DISCOMFORT OR PAIN ON THE OFFENDER.

HOWEVER, WITH *RESTORATIVE JUSTICE*, THE SENTIMENT IS THAT BECAUSE CRIME HURTS, JUSTICE SHOULD HEAL.

INSTEAD OF AN ADVERSARIAL COURT PROCEEDING, RESTORATIVE JUSTICE ENCOURAGES VICTIM-OFFENDER CONFERENCES WHERE THE STATE ACTS AS A MEDIATOR.

ADVOCATES OF RESTORATIVE JUSTICE PROPOSE THAT THE CRIMINAL SANCTION SHOULD DECREASE CRIME BY RESTORING:

THE VICTIM TO HER PREVIOUSLY UNHARMED STATUS AND--

--THE OFFENDER TO THE COMMUNITY.

MICHAEL, PLEASE DESCRIBE THE BEHAVIORS YOU ENGAGED IN.

WELL, I RELENTLESSLY STALKED HER. I MADE HER LIFE UNBEARABLE. I HURT HER AND HER FRIENDS.

IN THESE CONFERENCES, THE ACTIONS OF THE OFFENDER ARE CONDEMNED AND HE OR SHE IS ENCOURAGED TO TAKE RESPONSIBILITY, TO EXPRESS REMORSE, AND TO APOLOGIZE TO THE VICTIM. THE OFFENDER IS ALSO TREATED FAIRLY AND WITH RESPECT.

LAURIE, I'M SO SORRY I DID THAT. I KNOW IT WAS WRONG. I WON'T DO IT AGAIN.

THE VICTIM IS ALSO GRANTED THE OPPORTUNITY TO TELL THE OFFENDER HOW THE BEHAVIORS IMPACTED HIM OR HER.

I LIVED IN FEAR OF YOU. IT WAS SO OPPRESSIVE. I WASN'T ABLE TO LIVE MY LIFE.

THE GOAL IS TO SHAME THE CRIME BUT NOT THE CRIMINAL AND REINTEGRATE THE OFFENDER BACK INTO SOCIETY WITH PROPER SUPPORTS TO DO SO.

THIS PROVIDES A CIRCUMSTANCE IN WHICH THE OFFENDER CAN BE RESTORED TO SOCIETY WITHOUT THE STIGMATIZING LABEL ASSOCIATED WITH THE CRIMINAL BEHAVIOR.

ANOTHER POLICY INITIATIVE BASED ON REINTEGRATIVE SHAMING THAT CAN REDUCE THE NEGATIVE IMPACT SANCTIONS HAVE ON OFFENDERS IS *PRISON REENTRY PROGRAMS.*

INSTEAD OF ALLOWING INDIVIDUALS TO LEAVE PRISON WITH THEIR *CRIMINOGENIC NEEDS* UNTREATED, THEIR TIES TO FAMILY AND SUPPORT GROUPS WEAKENED, NO JOB PROSPECTS, NO PLACE TO LIVE, NO DRIVER'S LICENSE OR IDENTIFICATION...

...PRISON REENTRY PROGRAMS EMPHASIZE THE NEED TO START PREPARATION FOR REENTRY WHILE INDIVIDUALS ARE STILL IN PRISON, FOCUS ON CHALLENGES THEY MIGHT FACE IMMEDIATELY UPON RELEASE, AND PROVIDE SERVICES AND SUPPORT TO HELP REINTEGRATION BACK INTO THE COMMUNITY.

SINCE THE MAJORITY OF INDIVIDUALS WHO ARE IN PRISON WILL BE RELEASED, IT IS IMPORTANT THAT THEY LEAVE BETTER-- NOT WORSE--THAN WHAT THEY WERE WHEN THEY ENTERED THE INSTITUTION.

REENTRY PROGRAMS CAN HELP WITH THAT.

ANOTHER THING WE AS A SOCIETY CAN DO IS END THE USE OF NEGATIVE LABELS AND ADDRESS THESE INDIVIDUALS IN WAYS THAT ARE NOT AS HARMFUL OR JUDGMENTAL.

EXAMPLES INCLUDE: PERSON OR INDIVIDUAL WITH JUSTICE SYSTEM INVOLVEMENT; PERSON OR INDIVIDUAL PREVIOUSLY INCARCERATED; PERSON OR INDIVIDUAL ON PAROLE; PERSON OR INDIVIDUAL ON PROBATION; PERSON OR INDIVIDUAL IN DETENTION; PERSON WITH A HISTORY OF SUBSTANCE USE; OR BETTER YET--

DADDY! DADDY, I'M SO HAPPY YOU ARE GOING HOME WITH US!

THIS ISSUE INTRODUCED THE UNIQUE PERSPECTIVE OF LABELING THEORY. UNLIKE MOST CRIMINOLOGICAL THEORIES THAT FOCUS ON WHY AN INDIVIDUAL ENGAGES IN CRIMINAL BEHAVIOR OR HOW A SOCIAL ENVIRONMENT OR CIRCUMSTANCE CONTRIBUTES TO CRIME RATES, LABELING THEORY PROPOSES THAT WHAT CAUSES CRIME IS THE VERY THING THAT TRIES TO PREVENT IT: STATE INTERVENTION. LABELING THEORISTS CLAIM THAT STATE INTERVENTION IS "DANGEROUSLY CRIMINOGENIC" IN THAT THE LABELS WE PLACE ON INDIVIDUALS WHO COMMIT CRIMES CAN LEAD THEM TO CONTINUE TO ENGAGE IN CRIMINAL BEHAVIOR.

IN 1938, FRANK TANNENBAUM WROTE CRIME AND THE COMMUNITY TO DESCRIBE HIS THEORY OF "THE DRAMATIZATION OF EVIL." HE PROPOSES THAT AN ARREST SINGLES A PERSON OUT FOR DIFFERENTIAL TREATMENT AND EXPOSES HIM TO VARIOUS SYSTEMS AND CIRCUMSTANCES THAT OTHER INDIVIDUALS DO NOT EXPERIENCE. THE PERSON'S WORLD CHANGES, OTHERS REACT DIFFERENTLY TO HIM, AND HE BEGINS TO RECONSIDER HIS OWN IDENTITY. WHEN A PERSON IS GIVEN A NEGATIVE TAG OR LABEL, THIS OFTEN LEADS TO FUTURE DELINQUENT BEHAVIOR BECAUSE THE COMMUNITY REJECTS THE YOUTH, THE YOUTH BECOMES AWARE OF THE REJECTION, AND HE BEGINS TO IDENTIFY AS A DELINQUENT PERSON.

A LITTLE OVER A DECADE LATER, EDWIN LEMERT BUILT UPON TANNENBAUM'S IDEAS AND WROTE SOCIAL PATHOLOGY (1951). IN THIS WORK, HE DESIGNATED TWO TYPES OF DEVIANCE. PRIMARY DEVIANCE OCCURS WHEN A PERSON ENGAGES IN AN INITIAL ACT OF DEVIANCE. WHILE THIS BEHAVIOR ISN'T DESIRABLE, IT DOESN'T IMPACT THE PERSON'S STATUS OR SELF-IMAGE. THE PERSON DOESN'T SEE HIMSELF AS DEVIANT OR CRIMINAL AND DOESN'T ORGANIZE HIS LIFE AROUND THIS IDENTITY. SECONDARY DEVIANCE OCCURS WHEN OTHERS NEGATIVELY RESPOND TO THE PRIMARY DEVIANCE, AND THE SOCIETAL REACTION INTENSIFIES AS THESE ACTS CONTINUE. THE PERSON IS STIGMATIZED, AND HE REACTS TO THIS LABEL BY INCREASING HIS DEVIANT CONDUCT. SECONDARY DEVIANCE CAN BE SO STRONG THAT THE PERSON ADOPTS A MASTER STATUS.

POLICIES AND PROGRAMS THAT ARE BASED ON LABELING THEORY TRY TO DECREASE OR ELIMINATE STATE INTERVENTION. DECRIMINALIZATION CAN DECREASE STATE INTERVENTION BY REMOVING MANY FORMS OF CONDUCT FROM CRIMINAL LAW. DIVERSION PROGRAMS DIVERT INDIVIDUALS FROM THE CRIMINAL JUSTICE SYSTEM IN ORDER TO AVOID NEGATIVE CONSEQUENCES OF A CRIMINAL CONVICTION. ENSURING DUE PROCESS PROVIDES LEGAL PROTECTIONS FOR INDIVIDUALS WHO ARE ACCUSED OF CRIMES. DEINSTITUTIONALIZATION SEEKS TO REDUCE PRISON POPULATIONS SO THERE ARE FEWER INDIVIDUALS WHO ARE IMPACTED BY THE CRIMINOGENIC EFFECTS OF INCARCERATION.

JOHN BRAITHWAITE EXTENDED LABELING THEORY IN HIS WORK CRIME, SHAME AND REINTEGRATION (1989). HE DISCUSSED THE CONCEPT OF SHAME AND HOW THERE WERE TWO TYPES OF SHAMING. STIGMATIZATION OR DISINTEGRATIVE SHAMING IS CONSISTENT WITH LABELING THEORY, AS THE SHAMING STIGMATIZES AND EXCLUDES THE PERSON FROM THE COMMUNITY. IT IS DISRESPECTFUL AND TREATS THE INDIVIDUAL AS THOUGH HE OR SHE IS A BAD PERSON. REINTEGRATIVE SHAMING, ON THE OTHER HAND, INVOLVES EXPRESSING DISAPPROVAL WHILE SUSTAINING A RELATIONSHIP OF RESPECT AND LABELING THE BEHAVIOR AS DEVIANT, NOT THE INDIVIDUAL. THE BEHAVIOR IS ADDRESSED AND THEN THE PERSON IS REINTEGRATED BACK INTO THE COMMUNITY.

RESTORATIVE JUSTICE AND PRISON REENTRY PROGRAMS ARE INITIATIVES BASED IN REINTEGRATIVE SHAMING. RESTORATIVE JUSTICE ENCOURAGES VICTIM-OFFENDER CONFERENCES WHERE THE STATE ACTS AS A MEDIATOR, NOT AN ADVERSARY. THE ACTIONS OF THE OFFENDER ARE CONDEMNED, AND HE OR SHE IS ENCOURAGED TO TAKE RESPONSIBILITY AND MAKE AMENDS TO THE VICTIM AND THE COMMUNITY. PRISON REENTRY PROGRAMS PROVIDE OPPORTUNITIES FOR INCARCERATED INDIVIDUALS TO PREPARE FOR LIFE OUTSIDE OF THE INSTITUTION, FOCUS ON CHALLENGES UPON RELEASE, AND DISCOVER SERVICES AND SUPPORT TO HELP THEM REINTEGRATE BACK INTO THE COMMUNITY.

Key Terms

Labeling Theory
Frank Tannenbaum
The Dramatization of Evil
Tagging
Edwin Lemert
Primary Deviance
Secondary Deviance
Master Status
War on Poverty
Decriminalization
Legalization
Diversion
Specialty Courts
Treatment Courts
Problem-Solving Courts
Miranda Warning
Due Process
Deinstitutionalization
Brown v. Plata (2011)
John Braithwaite

Shame
Stigmatization
Disintegrative Shaming
Reintegrative Shaming
Restorative Justice
Prison Reentry Programs
Criminogenic Needs

Discussion Questions

1. Provide examples of five behaviors that were once legal but now criminal, or were once criminal but are now legal. Following from this, explain what it means that crime is "socially constructed." Does defining criminal behavior involve an objective or subjective process? Be thorough in your answer.

2. Would legalizing or decriminalizing drugs make it easier to treat individuals who abuse substances, or would it simply increase the number of substance abusers? Explain your reasoning.

3. Research specialty courts and/or problem-solving courts in your jurisdiction (city or county). Provide a detailed explanation of each type of court. Include in your answer who can participate, how an individual participates, other individuals or agencies that participate, the activities the individual engages in, and how the individual completes the court program.

4. What is the role of shame in the United States' criminal justice system today? Do you think reintegrative shaming can be applied to the United States' criminal justice system? Why or why not?

Suggested Readings

Braithwaite, J. (1989). *Crime, shame and reintegration*. Cambridge University Press.

Braithwaite, J. (2002). *Restorative justice and responsive regulation.* Oxford University Press.

Lemert, E. (1951). *Social pathology: A systemic approach to the theory of sociopathic behavior*. McGraw-Hill Book Company, Inc.

Lilly, J. R., Cullen, F. T., & Ball, R. A. (2019). *Criminological theory: Contexts and consequences* (7th ed.). Sage Publications.

Tannenbaum, F. (1938). *Crime and the community*. Columbia University Press.